INSPIRAT
MODULE ONI

CW00459452

ENROL HERE

FOR

PRACTITIONER

COURSE

www.innervisions.co.uk/practitioner

We build our reputation on your success

COPYRIGHT

ALL BOOKS, WRITTEN MATERIAL, PHOTOGRAPHS, AUDIOTRACKS, VIDEO'S, DVD'S AND OTHER MOVIES USED FOR THE DURATION OF THE COURSE ENTITLED

"A PRACTITIONER TRAINING IN CLINICAL HYPNOSIS"

ARE PROTECTED BY THE LAW OF COPYRIGHT.

NO PART OF MODULES ONE, TWO, THREE, FOUR, FIVE, SIX, SEVEN, EIGHT, NINE OR TEN OF THE COURSE NOTES AND OR COURSE LECTURES MAY BE RECORDED OR REPRODUCED BY ANY MECHANICAL, PHOTOGRAPHIC OR ELECTRONIC PROCESS, OR IN THE FORM OF A PHONOGRAPHIC RECORDING. NOR MAY IT BE STORED IN A RETRIEVAL SYSTEM, TRANSMITTED OR OTHERWISE COPIED FOR PUBLIC USE, INCLUDING TRAINING OF ANY THIRD PARTY, WITHOUT THE WRITTEN PERMISSION OF BRIAN GLENN.

INNERVISIONS SCHOOL OF CLINICAL HYPNOSIS WILL ENDEAVOUR TO TAKE LEGAL ACTION AGAINST ANY PERSON OR PERSONS OR ORGANISATIONS IN BREACH OF THIS COPYRIGHT STATEMENT NO MATTER HOW SMALL.

THE RECORDING OF STUDENT DEMONSTRATIONS IS STRICTLY FORBIDDEN

COPYRIGHT © BRIAN GLENN INNERVISIONS 2020 ONWARDS

DISCLAIMER

This book and its content does not provide medical advice and is not a substitute for medical advice or intervention.

The content is not intended to be a substitute for professional medical advice, diagnosis, or treatment. It is not a substitute for a medical examination, nor does it replace the need for services provided by a medical professional.

Always seek the advice of your medical professional before making any changes to your treatment. Any medical questions should be directed to your personal doctor.

Brian Glenn (the book author) or Innervisions School of Clinical Hypnosis makes no warranties, either expressed or implied concerning the accuracy, applicability, reliability or suitability of the contents of this book.

Brian Glenn (the book author) or Innervisions School of Clinical Hypnosis shall in no event be held liable for any direct, indirect incidental or other consequential damages arising directly or indirectly from any use of the information contained in this book.

All content is for information only and is not warranted for content accuracy or any other implied or explicit purpose.

CONTENTS

INTRODUCTION:

My name is Brian Glenn. In February 2021 I celebrated twenty-five years as a principal of Innervisions School of Clinical Hypnosis. I conducted my very first training course in the East Yorkshire town of Goole back in 1996

It actually all started about thirty years ago, when I changed direction and became a clinical hypnotherapist sparked by an amazing insight inspired by my father whilst performing my comedy hypnosis stage show on Blackpool Pier.

I had recently been disabled by an industrial injury where my dominant right arm was paralysed and withering away. My positive nature found a way to come to terms with my doctor's advice to amputate my arm, I was then actually looking forward to this in anticipation of being recognised as 'the one-armed hypnotist' – I even had posters printed!

My father commented on the power of the mind after attending my stage show and inspired me to use the power of my mind to repair my paralysed right arm. An amazing light bulb moment.

I studied the works of Milton Erickson MD who on two separate occasions used the power of his mind to learn to walk again following paralysis caused by polio.

The following twelve months was a turning point in my life as I used my skills to bring my arm back to around 95% recovery. I considered the industrial accident to be Karmic debt due to my rather aggressive and colourful teenage years, and spent time looking for a way to neutralise that debt. Then a few weeks later I woke in the earlier hours of the morning with an amazing inspirational and overwhelming message. It was in that moment that I made an agreement with myself which would eventually serve as my life's purpose whilst at the same time neutralise the Karmic debt I had accumulated as a teenager.

This was my revelation.

MY LIFE'S PURPOSE:
TO HELP ONE MILLION DURING MY LIFETIME

And so it began, my life became meaningful; for the first time in my life I had a sense of purpose. I abandoned stage hypnosis, attended a basic hypnotherapy training course and opened my first hypnotherapy clinic. I also enrolled on an 'A' level psychology course at my local college which eventually lead me to a degree in clinical psychology.

Miracles started to happen right before my eyes. I was seeing clients on a daily basis after opening a complimentary Health Centre on Hessle Road Hull.

Still not feeling like I was doing enough to achieve my 'Million', I decided to teach other people to do the work that I did creating a pyramid effect. This led to the birth of my training company: Innervisions School of Clinical Hypnosis.

Now semi-retired from hypnotherapy, and managing the business from our beautiful home in the Costa Blanca region of Spain, I am privileged and honoured to have a fantastic and wonderful team of dedicated tutors working at various venues around the UK and also here in Spain.

Behind the scenes, I have my wonderful and loving partner, Shirley, keeping me motivated and in good spirits doing all the business related stuff that I don't like doing!

Welcome to the fascinating and wonderful world of clinical hypnosis. I hope you enjoy the contents of this book!

Take care and stay safe. And perhaps one day soon you too could become part of my million!

With love...

Brian Glenn
PRINCIPAL
INNERVISIONS SCHOOL OF CLINICAL HYPNOSIS
www.innervisions.co.uk

PREFACE

Over the past twenty-five years, this hypnotherapy training course has evolved into one of Europe's most comprehensive resources for individuals looking to train in Modern Clinical Hypnosis.

We have a proven formula that will take you through a dedicated learning process using modern accelerated learning techniques, hosted by our world class tutors.

MODULAR TRAINING SYSTEM

The training consists of approximately 120 classroom training hours as specified by our accrediting body; The General Hypnotherapy Standards Council. In order to gain our diploma in clinical hypnosis and recommendation for full membership of GHSC, all course delegates must meet this requirement with no exceptions.

Students who are unable to attend any of the module dates will be given the opportunity to catch up on a one-to-one session with one of our tutors via Zoom. This will be a short version of the full weekend and an additional fee will be required due to extra tutor commitments. In order to comply with the GHSC training requirement of 120 classroom hours, students will only be allowed one, one-to-one Zoom catch up session.

MENTAL HEALTH ISSUES

It is your sole responsibility to inform your tutor of any known mental health issues which you are currently aware of now or during the whole of the training course. Information will be treated in strict confidence. In doing so we may need to exercise our duty of care and ask you to decline taking part in some of the exercises we demonstrate. If you are unsure, please speak to your tutor.

COURSE EVOLUTION

We are proud to be one of Europe's longest established training providers. Currently in our 25th year and still going strong.

This does not mean that we are still teaching the same course as we did all those years ago, indeed we update our course material and course content on every course intake.

Our tutors are constantly updating their knowledge and keeping up with major developments in the industry thus ensuring that the content always remains relevant, current and valid.

Post training, we have a unique and large hypnotherapy support community which is hosted by our private community Facebook page; all graduates will be added to this page post training.

Also, we have a unique one to one and/or peer group supervision service for all our graduates via zoom on a monthly basis. Details and dates are posted on our Facebook community page.

Furthermore, post training we offer our own in house exclusive CPD classes on various subjects which are promoted via our Facebook community page.

REFRESHER VIDEOS

We will be providing video tutorials of modules one to five with links to other videos and demonstrations.

These videos are for the sole use of past and present Innervisions students, and public distribution of any of the links on this page is strictly prohibited. Any breach of this condition will result in immediate expulsion from any further training and notification to GHSC.

In order to access the videos, please go on line to our website where you will find access to the modules after they are covered in class. www.innervisions.co.uk

Each module is password protected and the password for module one is:

sidney123

MODULE ONE

THE HISTORY OF HYPNOSIS

It is very important for you as a hypnotherapist to understand some of the history of hypnosis and the role of certain people who have helped hypnosis become the powerful tool that it is today.

The earliest references to hypnosis date back to ancient Egypt and Greece. Named after the Greek God of Sleep 'Hypnos'. Although the actual state of hypnosis is very different from that of sleep.

Both cultures had religious centres where people came for help with their problems. Hypnosis was used to induce dreams, which were then analysed to get to the root of the trouble. There are many references to trance and hypnosis in early writings. In 2600 BC the father of Chinese medicine, Wong Tai, wrote about techniques that involved incantations and passes of the hands. The Hindu Vedas written around 1500 BC mention hypnotic procedures. Trance-like states occur in many shamanistic, druidic, voodoo, yogic and religious practices.

HYPNOTIC PIONEERS

The father of hypnosis was an Austrian physician called **FRANZ MEZMER** (1734 - 1815), from whose name the word 'mesmerism is derived. He developed the theory of 'animal magnetism', the idea that diseases are the result of blockages in the flow of magnetic forces in the body. He believed that he could store his animal magnetism in large baths of iron filings and transfer it to patients with steel rods and 'mesmeric passes'.

The next pioneer of hypnosis was **JAMES BRAID** (1795 - 1860), a Scottish eye specialist who developed an interest in mesmerism purely by chance. One day, when he was late for an appointment, he found his patient in the waiting room staring into an old lamp with glazed eyes. Fascinated, Braid gave the patient some simple commands, telling him to close his eyes and go to sleep. The patient complied and Braid's interest grew. He discovered that getting patients to fixate on something was one of the most important elements in putting them into trance and he started to use a swinging watch as the eye fixation point. He subsequently published a book in which he proposed that the phenomenon be called 'hypnosis'.

Meanwhile, a British surgeon in India, **JAMES ESDAILE** (1805 - 1859), recognised the enormous benefits of hypnotism when used to relieve pain. He performed literally hundreds of major operations using hypnosis as the only form of anaesthetic. On returning to England the medical profession just laughed and ridiculed him. However, some people say that if chloroform had not been discovered around the same time as hypnosis for anaesthesia, then hypnosis would be more widely used today.

Another pioneer was the Frenchman **EMILE COUE** (1857 - 1926). He developed something called 'auto suggestion', although he is perhaps even more famous for his saying "Every day in every way I am getting better and better". His new technique was the affirmation technique. He also anticipated what is known as the placebo effect. Recent research into placebos is quite startling and shows that placebos often work better than conventional medicine. Emile Coue was the first person to realise the power of suggestion in hypnosis.

Emile Coue began to study suggestibility and this led to a major breakthrough in the history of hypnosis. He went on to develop the three laws of suggestion.

THE THREE LAWS OF SUGGESTION

THE LAW OF CONCENTRATED ATTENTION

According to the law of concentrated attention, when a person concentrates his or her attention on an idea, that idea tends to become reality. As the Bible says: "As man thinketh... so he becomes."

THE LAW OF REVERSE EFFORT

The law of reverse effect means that when a person thinks s/he cannot do something and then tries, the more s/he tries to do it, the less able s/he is to do it.

THE LAW OF DOMINANT EFFECT

This means that a suggestion linked to an emotion will override any other suggestion in the person's mind at the time. The dominating affect (emotion) connected to that suggestion causes it to have a stronger influence on the mind.

SIGMUND FREUD (1856 - 1939) was also interested in hypnosis, initially using it extensively in his work. He eventually abandoned his practice for a number of reasons, the most important being that he was not successful. He favoured psychoanalysis, a kind of hypnotherapy but without hypnosis.

In more recent times, one of the most famous authorities on clinical hypnosis was the psychotherapist **MILTON ERICKSON** (1901-1980). As a teenager he was stricken with polio and paralysed, but he managed to re-mobilise himself. It was while paralysed that he began to observe and analyse people, and he became fascinated by human psychology. Erickson treated people by using techniques such as metaphor, confusion and humour, while they were in a hypnotic trance. He became famous for his 'indirect techniques'. Today a hypnotherapist who uses indirect suggestions is deemed to be an 'Ericsonian'.

During your training we will teach you a mixture of direct and indirect techniques.

EXPLANATION OF HYPNOSIS

In order to allay some of the fears and misconceptions about hypnosis, It is important to stress that what takes place under hypnosis is safe, natural, non-magical, and produces very predictable results.

There is absolutely no question of being controlled or manipulated, or even induced into a hypnotic state against your will. People in hypnosis are not "asleep". On the contrary, they are often more aware than usual of what is taking place, and their senses function far more efficiently than normal. People cannot be made to do anything that they do not want to do. People who say or think, "Nobody can get me under", "I wouldn't want anybody controlling my mind" or who say "But I might blurt all my secrets out", are simply demonstrating that they have a total misconception of what hypnosis really is.

The state of hypnosis, which is a totally natural phenomenon, is very pleasant and very relaxing. Under hypnosis people can converse very easily. It is impossible for them to come to any harm. Indeed, the centuries-old technique of hypnosis is being used increasingly as an adjunct to orthodox medicine. It is proving a valuable alternative to drugs for anaesthesia, and has been found to accelerate healing, accelerate learning, relieve stress, control pain and increase performance.

DEFINITION OF HYPNOSIS

The definition of hypnosis is

"A state of focused attention with heightened awareness and increased suggestibility"

We, as clinical hypnotherapists, have only ever hypnotised one person. All hypnosis is self-hypnosis and a hypnotherapist is merely a facilitator who uses techniques to help clients into self-hypnosis, and then to facilitate a positive change in behaviour.

It is for this reason that no one could possibly be hypnotised against his or her will. In order for any hypnotherapist, or stage hypnotist to hypnotise another person, FULL co-operation is required at all times.

CAN ANYONE BE HYPNOTISED?

You bet! In fact, every human being goes in and out of hypnosis all day long. Here are several examples of going into hypnosis on a daily basis.

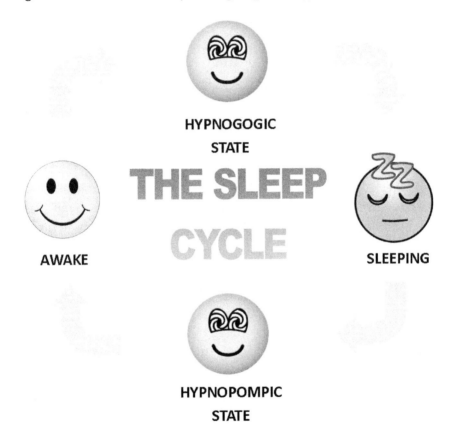

HYPNOGOGIC STATE

THE SLEEP CYCLE

AWAKE

SLEEPING

HYPNOPOMPIC STATE

When humans decide it's time to go to sleep, they usually go to bed in the fully awake state; the state they are in most of the day. After climbing into bed they gently drift into a hypnotic state called the 'hypnogogic' state. After a short while, they drift off to sleep.

Then just prior to waking they gently drift into another hypnotic state called the 'hypnopompic' state. And soon after that they return back to the fully awaken state, ready to face the day ahead.

Humans are the only species that actually do this, it's an important part of their stress relief mechanism which we discuss a little more on module two.

Most other animals, your cat for example, can instantly flit between sleep and awake randomly without any problems.

LONG DISTANCE DRIVING

You may have experienced this when driving a long way on a route that you know well. All of a sudden you think to yourself, "I can't remember passing a certain bridge," or "I don't remember going through the traffic lights at x". Yet all the time you are in this state of trance, you are still in full control of the vehicle.

TRAFFIC LIGHTS

Have you ever stopped at a red light and started to stare at it in anticipation of it changing to green, then something pops into your mind, you go into hypnosis and the lights change to green and although you are still looking at the traffic light, you don't actually notice that it's changed to green! – The car behind you sounds its horn to bring you out of trance!

READING A BOOK

When you read fiction or a novel, you lose all awareness of the people and the room around you. You become so engrossed that you are actually "in there" with the people in the story.

WATCHING TELEVISION

You may have been looking at the television screen for the past 20 minutes, yet you have no idea of what was going on. Your mind has drifted away to somewhere else. All of a sudden you wake and think "Oh God, I missed that bit", yet all the time you were actually looking at the screen.

REMINISCING & DAYDREAMING

When we start to reminisce about a past traumatic or fantastic experience, we actually forget about where we currently are and what we are doing. We tend to go back and revisit these times with almost the same emotional charge as we experience when it actually happened. After a while we 'snap' out of it and continue with our daily routine.

It's interesting to point out that when we do this, sometimes our physical bodies act like it's really happening and display physical signs. For example if we sit down and start to imagine ghosts and spooky things, our skin will soon produce 'goose pimples' and shivers!

COMMON QUESTIONS AND ANSWERS

The most common question people ask is:

"What if I don't wake up?"

Saying this to a hypnotist is rather like saying, "I won't wash my hair because what if it doesn't dry". In other words, this scenario is just not possible. If after putting someone into a hypnotic trance, the hypnotist for some reason drops dead, one of two things will happen:

1. The subject will immediately wake up or "shock waken";
2. The subject will fall into a normal sleep and wake when s/he is ready.

There is absolutely NO chance of anyone being "locked" in hypnosis for ever.

"Can everyone be hypnotised?"

Yes, every human being can be hypnotised with the following three exceptions:

- Young children under about 5
- Severely mentally disturbed
- People who choose not to be hypnotised

People do go into different depths of hypnosis, but hypnotherapy can be of benefit to everyone.
"Will I blurt out all my personal secrets?"

No, you will always be in full control of everything you say and do. There is no question of being in the power of the hypnotist and made to do things you don't want to do.

"Will I actually be sleeping?"

No, you will not be asleep or awake, but somewhere in the middle. You will be in a state in which all your natural senses will be around 30% more efficient than usual. You will be **FULLY AWARE** of what is going on at **ALL** times.

"When in hypnosis, will I do things against my will?"

Certainly **NOT!** A person in hypnosis is in **TOTAL CONTROL** of the situation at **ALL** times.

Although the word "sleep" is used frequently in hypnosis, a person in hypnosis is not actually asleep. In fact s/he is neither wide-awake nor asleep, but somewhere "in between".

THE AMAZING HUMAN MIND

The human mind is rather like an iceberg, in that most people only see the tip. The human mind consists of two parts, the conscious and the subconscious. Most people are aware of the 20% that is the conscious mind but there is another 80% underneath which has an amazing potential, and is often not used as well as it perhaps could be.

THE CONSCIOUS MIND

CHARACTERISTICS OF THE CONSCIOUS MIND

The conscious mind is relatively weak. It makes us human and gives us the ability to predict things, and has a strong sense of time.

The conscious mind:

- Apparently controlled by the left part of the brain (logic)
- Always analyses and criticises
- Applies logic
- Has a sense of humour
- Its language is verbal
- Short term memories
- Seven plus minus two rule (Millers magic)
- Chunking

THE SUBCONSCIOUS MIND

The subconscious mind contains all your wisdom, memories and intelligence. It is responsible for all the things that you *don't* have to think about. These include:

- Blood pressure
- Heartbeat rate
- Breathing rate
- Body temperature
- Things you have been trained to do
- Memories
- And lots more...

CHARACTERISTICS OF THE SUBCONSCIOUS MIND

The subconscious mind:

- Apparently controlled by the right part of the brain (creative)
- Cannot analyse and criticise
- Takes every piece of information literally
- Cannot distinguish between pretend and real
- Has no sense of humour
- Its language is the imagination
- Main function is to protect the owner
- Will run all programmes it considers protective
- Never forgets
- Lives in the now with no sense of time

HOW DOES HYPNOSIS WORK?

Whilst a person is in hypnosis, the hypnotherapist is able to communicate directly with the subconscious part of his or her mind. This is the part that does things that people don't have to think about (e.g., their breathing). Since the subconscious mind does not analyse nor criticise anything that is said to it, it will accept as literal *almost* anything that is said, and will do this automatically without the person even knowing.

So, for example, if you wanted to stop smoking, the hypnotist would put you into hypnosis, and then communicate with the subconscious part of your mind.

Basically, s/he would use the power of *suggestion* to tell your subconscious mind that you will never want to smoke again. Your subconscious mind will accept this and will carry out the instructions. As a consequence of this, because you have put these suggestions into the part of the mind that does everything automatically, you won't even want to smoke.

A good example of the conscious and subconscious mind is as follows.

When you are learning to do something, for example, drive a car, you are using your conscious mind. You may think "blimey, I'll never remember all this", but once you have taken your examination or passed your driving test, then all of a sudden, things seem to come more easily. You seem to go onto "auto pilot".
This is because with practice, all the information has now been passed on to the subconscious mind, so that you no longer have to think about what you are doing.

Remember how difficult it was when you were learning to ride a bike, and compare this with how easy it is now!

THE POWER OF SUGGESTION

Every single day of our lives we are open to the overwhelming power of suggestion. This is what makes us the person we are, from the day we are born to the way we are today.

Here are several simple examples of the power of suggestion in the waking state or, if you like, the normal state without hypnosis.

1. Remember the girl at school who would start to blush when anyone said forcefully, "Oh look, she's starting to blush".

2. When you are with a friend, start to scratch various places on your body, and guess what? Yes that's right, your friend starts to itch. Simply mention fleas or something, and again they will start to itch.

3. When you are with a group of friends, start to yawn... then watch *them* yawn!

This next little story illustrates the power of suggestion well...

Imagine, if you will, that we have a long plank of wood about one foot wide and twelve feet long. We place it on the floor and then walk along it from one end to the other. You can do this easily and keep your balance perfectly. But now let's say we take this plank and place it high up in the air, for example between two very tall buildings. Can you walk over it now like you did before? Most people will refuse even to try. Why? After all, you have just walked along the very same board from one end to the other, without the slightest difficulty, so why the hesitation now just because it has been elevated? The matter of balance is still the same. However, it is just as well that you refuse to walk along the board, in this new dangerous position, as the chances are that you would become dizzy, probably fall off, and perhaps even kill yourself. So why is this? The answer is simple. The position of the board now stretched out at a great height, suggests the possibility of a fall. The suggestion of falling is now present. You have suggested to yourself that you may fall off and kill yourself. This suggestion is so powerful that in fact it interferes with your sense of balance and, try as you will; you will not overcome this suggestion (fear) of a dangerous fall – unless, of course, you belong to a circus!

WHY DOES HYPNOSIS WORK?

The answer in one word is **suggestion.** We know that the mind is open to receiving suggestions.

We know that suggestion has made us who and what we are. We also know that suggestion can change us for good or evil. When we are born, we all have a blank mind and a brain like a sponge.

We have no experience. Apart from the fear of falling and a fear of loud noises, babies are virtually free of all fear. Apart from food, babies have no desires, no compulsions, and no phobias.

When we are born, we do not know what a cigarette or a spider is. We have no fear of the dark, no fear of open or enclosed spaces. We are born without any prejudices. We do not hate, and we do not love. We do not need a car, a television, or new clothes.

We are not jealous; we do not lust, and we do not need sex. We possess none of the seven deadly sins. As we go through life's experiences, the pages of our diary are gradually filled in as we use all of our five senses - touch, taste, sight, hearing and smell.

So, what you are today is a result of all your accumulated experiences from the day you were born right up to this very minute. And in ten years from now you will be a different person, you will have changed. Did you ever suggest to your children that if they 'eat it all up', they will grow up to be a big girl/boy?

If your partner tells you that you are useless, how does it make you feel... useless?

Now stop reading this and stare at the picture below for a few minutes and notice what happens...

Did it make you feel hungry or did you start to salivate? Did it make you feel sick? It probably made a very powerful suggestion to you in some positive or negative way.

Can you remember this old TV advert?

Hmmm, great example of the Law of Dominant Effect. This advert was eventually banned for invoking the 'wrong emotions' ☺

PERCEPTION

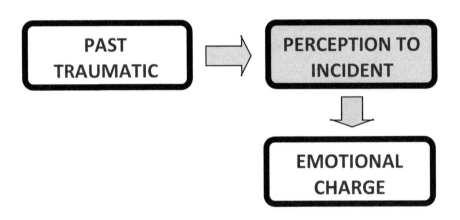

Most psychosomatic problems have their roots in the past. Most memories are permanent and cannot be erased.

A 'perception' to a distant memory can have a very powerful effect on a person in their daily lives.

Fortunately, we all as human beings, perceive things differently, and a past trauma in one person's life may not even be affecting them in the now, simply because that person has a different perception to others.

However, a person suffering from a past memory will normally have a very strong perception to the incident in the now, which will often leave that person highly emotionally charged and open to lots of different types of psychosomatic illnesses and life problems.

We can't change the past!

BUT WE CAN CHANGE OUR PERCEPTION TO THE PAST

This will substantially decrease the emotional charge and enhance the quality of the person's life.

Basically, if you can change a person's perception of a negative memory, then the emotional charge will change accordingly!

All hypnosis is about changing a person's perception to something, stage hypnotists do it all the time!!!

BASIC PRESUPPOSITIONS

1.   THE MIND MAP IS NOT A TERRITORY

Our mental maps of OUR world are not THE world. We respond to our maps, rather than the world. Mental maps, especially feelings and interpretations, can be updated far more easily than the world can be changed.

2.   ALL EXPERIENCE HAS A STRUCTURE

Our thoughts and memories have a pattern to them. When we change a pattern or structure, our experience will automatically change. We can neutralise unpleasant memories and enrich memories that will serve us.

3.   IF ONE PERSON CAN DO SOMETHING, ANYONE CAN LEARN TO DO IT

We can learn an achiever's mental map and make it our own. Too many people think that things are impossible without even going out and trying them. Pretend that everything is possible. When there are environmental or physical limits, the world of experience will let you know about it.

PREMATURE COGNITIVE CONDITIONING

When an Indian elephant is born, the keepers will chain the small elephant to a large tree. After about one year, the chain is swapped for a flimsy rope fastened to the tree. At any time, the elephant could simply and easily break the rope or even pull the tree out of the ground. The adult elephant will never even attempt to break the rope. "WHY NOT?"

The answer is simple; the elephant does not believe it can and therefore does not even attempt to escape!

FIRST YEAR OF LIFE   REST OF ELEPHANTS LIFE

An interesting thing happens if you introduce young fish to a tank, partitioning the tank in the middle with and dividing the fish equally on each side of the partition. After approximately one month, if you were to remove the partition, the fish will not go past where that partition was.

This is simply because they do not know that they can! This principal is called "premature cognitive commitment", basically, the Elephant has "prematurely" meaning "too early", "cognitively", made a commitment to itself that it cannot break the rope, and therefore does not even attempt to do so.

Does this process sound familiar? Human beings frequently do this. We become a victim of our own beliefs. If we believe we cannot do something, we don't even attempt to do it!
Most people have potential that is locked away for ever; simply because they have prematurely cognitively committed themselves to not doing things.

Back to the Presuppositions:

4.   THE MIND AND BODY ARE PART OF THE SAME SYSTEM

Our thoughts instantly affect our muscle tension, breathing, feelings and more, and these in turn affect our thoughts. When we learn to change either one, we have learned to change the other.

5.   PEOPLE ALREADY HAVE THE RESOURCES THEY NEED

Mental images, inner voices, sensations and feelings are the basic building blocks of all our mental and physical resources. We can use them to build any thought, feeling, or skill we want, and then place them in our lives where we want them and need them most.

6.   YOU CANNOT <u>NOT</u> COMMUNICATE

We are always communicating, at least non verbally, and words are often the least important part. A sigh, a smile or a look are all communications. Even our thoughts are communications to ourselves and they are revealed to others through our eyes, voice tone,   and posture and body movements.

7.   UNDERLYING EVERY BEHAVIOUR THERE IS POSITIVE INTENT

Every harmful, hurtful or even thoughtless behaviour had a positive response in its original situation; yelling in order to be acknowledged; hitting to fend off anger; hiding to feel safe. Rather than condoning or condemning these actions, we can separate them from the person's positive intent, so that new, updated and more positive choices can be added that mean the same intent.

8.   PEOPLE ARE ALWAYS MAKING THE BEST CHOICE(S) AVAILABLE TO THEM

Every one of us have our own unique personal history. Within it, we learned what to do and how to do it, what to value and how to value it, what to learn and how to learn it. This is our experience. From it we must make all our choices; that is until new and better ones are added.

9.   IF WHAT YOU ARE DOING IS NOT WORKING, DO SOMETHING ELSE

If you always do what you have always done, you will always get what you have always got. If you want something new, **_do_** something new; especially when there are many alternatives.

10.   THE QUALITY OF LIFE IS ONLY AS GOOD AS THE QUALITY OF YOUR THOUGHTS

It has been scientifically proven that when we think pleasant things, our bodies produce chemicals which improve our immune system, and make us feel good. When we are "thinking" about something, we are actually practising the science of "brain chemistry".

WHO'S IN CONTROL?

Most people have many misconceptions regarding what hypnosis really is. The most common misconception is that a hypnotist or a hypnotherapist has the ability to control people.

In reality, if this was true, there would be no stage hypnotists or hypnotherapists. Hypnotists would probably not be interested in the welfare of people or even performing on stage, they would in fact be making lots of money, perhaps even running the country.

So, why is it then that people on stage behave in an 'apparently' bazaar way. They appear to be under the control of the hypnotist.

Let's explain how this works in a stage setting, then we can relate this to therapy, and then to the individual client.

STAGE HYPNOSIS

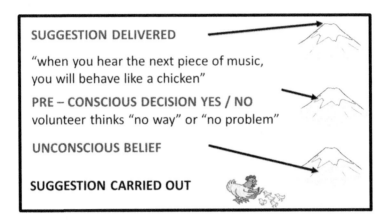

Let's suppose that Fred and Joe Bloggs decide to volunteer to take part in a stage show. The hypnotist would put them both into deep trance. Now, remember that Fred and Joe are two completely different people with their own unique personality and codes of ethics. The hypnotist could now go to Fred and say, "as soon as I click my fingers, you will be a chicken", Fred thinks to himself, "there is no way I am going to make a fool of myself in this theatre", the hypnotist clicks his fingers and nothing happens! (Fred rejected the suggestion; however, he remains in hypnosis)

He then says to Joe, "as soon as I click my fingers, you will be a chicken", Joe, who has a different personality to Fred thinks "ok, it's Friday night, let's have some fun, I trust this hypnotist and its only harmless fun".

Now, simply because Joe has accepted this suggestion and considers it just harmless fun, the suggestion now filters through to the subconscious where it now becomes reality. So from now on, every time the hypnotist clicks his fingers, Joe has an uncontrollable urge to behave like a chicken!

THERAPY

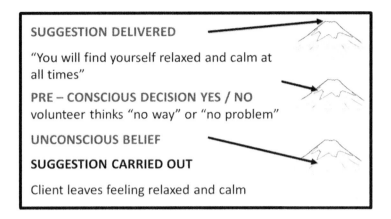

SUGGESTION DELIVERED

"You will find yourself relaxed and calm at all times"

PRE – CONSCIOUS DECISION YES / NO
volunteer thinks "no way" or "no problem"

UNCONSCIOUS BELIEF

SUGGESTION CARRIED OUT

Client leaves feeling relaxed and calm

If you have a client, and s/he was in hypnosis, and you were to say something like "when you leave this building, you will jump under the first red bus that you see", s/he would probably reject the suggestion and when s/he leaves the building, nothing will happen.

However, if you were to say something like "when you leave this building, you will feel wonderful", s/he is more likely to accept this suggestion and it would then filter through to the subconscious and become reality.

THE 'UNIQUE' CLIENT

Because each client is unique, they will never accept a suggestion that is not good for them. Also, if your client has any doubts about any changes they claim to want to make, then s/he will simply reject the suggestion. Always remember that a suggestion that may sound perfect to you may not be perfect to the client, and therefore may be rejected.

It is obvious then that hypnosis is in fact about control, but not on the hypnotist's behalf. The client always remains in control and will always reject suggestions that s/he feels are inappropriate.

SENSORY SYSTEMS

We take in information about the world we live in through our five senses. The use of these five senses is called the VAKOG system.

V = VISUAL = TO SEE

A = AUDITORY = TO HEAR

K = KINAESTHETIC = TO FEEL

O = OLFACTORY = TO SMELL

G = GUSTATORY = TO TASTE

We also use three of these sensory systems to induce hypnosis. The induction we will use today is called the VAK (visual, auditory, kinaesthetic) trance induction.

RAPPORT

The rapport building skills we are about to teach you are all natural techniques that all human beings use on a daily basis. We normally do this selectively. We will be in rapport with the people that we like and out of rapport with those we don't like. When we understand the basic dynamics of rapport, we can use these skills to communicate effectively with almost anyone.

Salesmen use rapport building techniques all the time. In order to turn a potential customer into an actual customer they need to have some kind of rapport with their client. You could have the world's best product, but if the customer does not like you, it is unlikely that he will buy from you. On the other hand, you could be selling the world's worst product, and if your customer is in rapport with you, he will like you so much, that he finds it hard to say "no".

We need rapport in order to:

- To get a person to "level off" with you

- To get a person into your mode of thinking

- To get a person to trust you without asking him to

- To get a subconscious link with another person

- To get a person to behave in a way you want him to without realising it

- Make it difficult for the subconscious to resist desired outcome.

As a hypnotherapist it is very important to gain rapport with our clients, this way the client will trust you and work with you.

Over the coming months, we will be teaching you the basics of rapport building, and then taking it a step further, where we can use various techniques to gain "rapid rapport".

If you are wondering what the "key" to a successful induction is, then here it is. Get this right and you are 90% there!

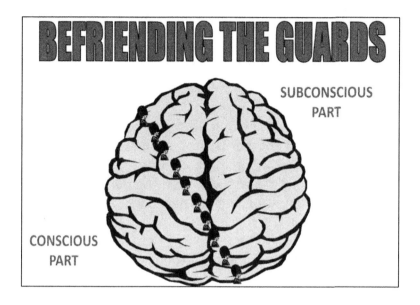

The only way we can befriend these guards is to get good rapport. The first thing you need to learn to do is to befriend those "guards" and get them to "trust" you. The more guards you get down, the further the person will go into hypnosis. It is highly unlikely that you will ever get all the guards down because you will need 100% trust and this may be a little too much to expect from any client.

It is essential for the therapist to begin to develop some form of rapport with the client right from their first meeting. Rapport can be developed in many ways.

If your client resists entering trance, it is usually because there is lack of rapport.

BASIC RAPPORT BUILDING

EYE CONTACT

Appropriate eye contact is usually the most important way of communicating one's full and undivided attention. It can easily be achieved by doing the following.

1.   Focus your eyes on the other person and gently shift your gaze from his or her face to another part of the body, such as a gesturing hand or a tapping foot, then back to the face and to the eyes. Occasionally moving your gaze away from the person will reduce the chance of staring or of causing him or her to feel anxiety or suspicion. Let yourself be natural.

2.   Avoid staring at the person or feigning eye contact by fixing your eyes on the person's forehead. These behaviours can be mistaken for doubt, hostility or insincerity.

3.   Avoid looking away from your client for long periods. If you are distracted by turning your gaze to others as they walk by, or by noises in the environment, the other person may interpret this as lack of interest.

NON-VERBAL PROMPTS

These demonstrate listening, and also encourage the person to continue speaking.

1.   **Affirmative head nodding.**
        These head nods should be used occasionally and paired with eye contact.

2.   **Appropriate facial expressions.**
        Generally, your facial expressions should reflect the nature and intensity of the person's expressed feelings, rather than your own reactions to them. A frown is appropriate if you do not follow or understand a person's point.

3.   **The use of silence.**
        Silence on the part of the therapist can communicate patience, and prompt the client to start speaking in order to break the silence.

OPEN BODY POSTURE

Relaxing your own body will usually encourage the client to relax also. When your body shows openness and receptivity, the other person is likely to talk freely and be less defensive. You can achieve open body posture in the following ways.

1.   Face the person, rather than sitting or standing at his or her side.

2.   Uncross your arms and legs. Crossed arms can communicate superiority or defensiveness, as well as serving as a barrier.

3.   Lean slightly forward. This communicates interest. Slouching is an indication of boredom, fatigue or lack of interest.

BODY LANGUAGE

MATCHING

A good way to "match" people initially is the use of body language. This involves matching the client's body posture. It's a well-known fact that when people are together, particularly couples in a social situation, they mirror and match one another. They do this subconsciously, but it makes them feel at ease with each other. Hand movements and facial expressions when matched also help with rapport building.

MISMATCHING

On the other hand, by deliberately mismatching the client, the therapist can break rapport. This can be used at the end of a therapy session, say with a persistently chatty client.

MATCHING AND MIRRORING

Matching is the duplication of a client's movements. Mirroring is simply the mirroring of their posture.

DESCRIBING HYPNOSIS

Describing hypnosis to the client and correcting any misconceptions that they may have about it helps to build rapport.

It's amazing the misconceptions that clients can have, and yet they are so desperate to get treatment for their problems, that they are still prepared to "give it a try".

ANSWERING CLIENTS' QUESTIONS

It is always a good idea to let the clients ask questions about hypnosis, as this often reveals the particular aspects of hypnosis that are worrying them.

EXPLANATION OF HYPNOSIS

A good explanation of hypnosis and what the client can expect is, I believe, essential, because of the many different preconceived ideas about hypnosis. For instance, clients may believe that in hypnosis they will not be able to hear anything and that they will go into oblivion. This is not so of course, and should be pointed out.

THE HYPNOTIC VOICE

New students of hypnotherapy need to develop their hypnotic voice. This can only develop with practice. It means slowing down your speech to about half its normal speed, deepening the tonality and speaking quietly. The way you speak is anchored to the trance experience.

When the client arrives for further therapy at a later date and you change to your hypnotic voice, s/he will want to go into hypnosis.

SIGNS OF HYPNOSIS

As the client starts to relax, the therapist should be able to see the difference in breathing rate.

Other signs to look for are fluttering eyelids, closing of the eyes, signs of profound relaxation, the smoothing of facial muscles, and excessive salivation or swallowing. You will be able to see facial expressions relevant to the suggestions being made. Your client may turn pale due to a drop in blood pressure. Head movements and motor signals will be very slight.

In the Progressive Relaxation Technique, you can start by suggesting relaxation of the muscles from the head all the way down to the tips of the toes or, if you prefer, the other way round.

IMPORTANT NOTE

If you do **not** get any of the above signs, do **not** assume that your client is **not** in hypnosis as they probably are!

ALWAYS ASSUME THAT YOUR CLIENT **IS** IN HYPNOSIS.

YOUR FIRST HYPNOTIC INDUCTION

CAUTION

Please <u>DO NOT</u> attempt to carry out this powerful hypnotic procedure without attending Module 1. INNERVISIONS, bears no responsibility should you choose to do so.

STAGE 1 - BUILDING CONFIDENCE

Before you attempt to put your first volunteer into hypnosis, I want to stress that this first rapport-building section is extremely important, and the success of your first induction depends on this first phase.

- Explain to your volunteer exactly what to expect and how s/he will feel

- Deal with any myths, fears, and misconceptions

- Mirror & match client

- Explain what hypnosis is, and isn't

- Explain functions of conscious and subconscious

- Explain how we get unwanted behaviours

- Ask client if they have any questions before you hypnotise him/her

STAGE 2 - TRANCE INDUCTION

Remember that a person in hypnosis has NO sense of time, so if you get stuck for words, just stop, relax and think... You will get bored before your client does!

SPEAK SLOWLY AND RHYTHMICALLY

First I would like you to find a small spot on the wall or ceiling.

Now stare at that spot and don't move your attention or gaze from it. Really concentrate on that spot. Check out the size... Shape... Colour... Really focus all your attention on that spot... Look at it, stare at it until your eyes feel tired. Continue looking, gazing and concentrating. Maybe it might go blurred, or change shape or colour... I don't really know, but for now just stare at it and concentrate on it. You may start to blink a little, that's ok. Just continue to look at that spot...

Now when I count to three, I would like you to close your eyes and imagine that you can still see that spot, but it won't matter if you can't see it, just imagine that you can.

1...   2...   3...

Keep telling the client how well s/he is doing.

Pause for three seconds...

Now use your ears and listen. Listen to all the tiny sounds around you.

Pause for three seconds...

Now I would like you to feel how your hands feel as they are resting on your knees.

Pause for three seconds...

Now I would like you to feel how your feet feel as they are resting on the floor. Maybe they feel heavy or perhaps they feel light... I don't know, only you know exactly how they feel.

Pause for three seconds...

Now I would like you to focus on your back resting against the chair...

Pause for three seconds...

I wonder if you've noticed how your breathing has already started to slow down... This is what happens when you start to relax... your breathing starts to slow down, and the more it slows down, the more you relax... and the more you relax, the more your breathing slows down.

Pause for three seconds...

And now you can open your eyes again and stare at the same spot. This time you will notice that it is different... Maybe the spot is becoming blurred and perhaps a little out of focus. Your eyes are getting a little tired and you may find that they start to blink a bit. And this time you will find that, by the time I count to three, you will just want to close your eyes and relax, and that you will feel very relaxed indeed.

So here we go then... 1... 2... 3... Now gently close your eyes and relax.

Pause for three seconds...

Now use your ears and listen. Listen to all the tiny sounds around you.

Pause for three seconds...

Now I would like you to feel how your hands feel as they are resting on your knees.

Pause for three seconds...

Now I would like you to feel how your feet feel as they are resting on the floor. Maybe they feel heavy or perhaps they feel light... I don't know, only you know exactly how they feel.

Pause for three seconds...

Now I would like you to focus on your back resting against the chair.

Pause for three seconds...

You may have noticed how your breathing has started to slow down even more...   This is what happens when you start to relax...   your breathing starts to slow down, and the more it slows down, the more you relax...   and the more you relax, the more your breathing slows down.

STAGE 3 - RELAXING THE BODY (optional)

From now on, all the sounds around you will be of no use to you anymore. Although you can still hear them, they will be of no use to you anymore.

The only sound that you will be interested in from now on is the sound of my voice...   the warm, comforting sound of my voice...   And every word that I speak will sound comforting and relaxing to you.

Now I am going to help you to relax the whole of your body, little by little, muscle by muscle, and it will be so easy for you to do this.

All you have to do is listen to the sound of my voice, and think about each muscle as I mention it, and you will be pleasantly surprised at just how easily and quickly you start to relax.

First I am going to start with the muscles in your face, and then work my way down so that your whole body is relaxed, right down to the tips of your toes.

Now think about the muscles around your eyes and, as you think about them, just let them relax.

Give your client time to think about each muscle before moving on to the next.

Now to the muscles in your cheeks...

Now the muscles in your lips and jaw, just allow them to do as they will.

Now to your neck and shoulders, just let your shoulders fall...

Continue working your way down the body, mentioning all the muscles.

And there you are, completely relaxed and at ease.

And now I would like you to just hold on to this feeling of relaxation for a minute or two. I am going to go silent for a few moments so that you can enjoy this special feeling of peace and relaxation.

STAGE 4 – CONFIDENCE BOOSTER

The dotted parts are 'one second' speech gaps, and the Bold words should be emphasized using your voice.

Now that you're **so deeply** relaxed...   your mind has become extremely sensitive...   and so receptive to what I am saying...   therefore, all the suggestions and thoughts I put to you...   which **are all for your own good**...   you can allow to sink **deeply** into your subconscious mind...   **so deeply** in fact that you can keep them there for as long as you need them, and because they are **so firmly** and **so deeply** imbedded in your subconscious mind you can become aware of changes taking place.

Maybe now that you're so **relaxed**... you can realise that **everything** I say from now on... is going to help you to become that wonderful person you want to be. ...So, during this **wonderful** state of **relaxation** that you are in... you can start to feel physically **stronger** and **fitter** in every way... you can feel **more alert**... **more wide-awake** ... and more **energetic.** You can start to feel good all around... and as each day goes by... allow yourself to become so deeply interested in what you are doing ---- allow yourself these things and notice how **much better** it makes you feel.

Enjoy these new feelings; enjoy the **changes** they bring with them... and these **changes**... will... I am

sure, continue every day just like a snowball...
getting bigger and bigger... **steadier** and **steadier**...
so big... so **steady**... that your nerves will also want
to be **steadier** and **stronger** and then your mind can
become **calmer** and **clearer**... more **composed**...
peaceful... more **tranquil**.

All these changes can start to take place as soon as
your subconscious mind allows them to, helping you
to see things in their true perspective and **coping**
better than you've been able to cope for a long time.

You can be pleasantly surprised about this and even
wonder about it... however just let it all happen. You
can wonder at how **relaxed** and **calm** you are starting
to feel as each day goes by... These things will
happen all by themselves... just let them happen.
And as you become more and more **relaxed** and **calm**

each day... you can be aware of developing much more **confidence** in yourself... more confidence in your ability to do... just what you'd like to do... lots of **confidence**... to do the things you'd like to do... whatever it may be... because of this... every day... you can feel more and more **independent**... more able to stick up for yourself... to stand on your own two feet... to hold your own... no matter how difficult or trying it may be.

From this day onwards be aware of the greater feelings of **personal wellbeing**... a greater feeling **of personal safety**... and **security**... than you've felt for a long time... and because all these things are beginning to happen... because changes are about to take place... **exactly** as you would like them to... only more and more **quickly**... **powerfully**... and **completely**... as each day goes by... you can now feel **much happier**... much more **contented**... **much more optimistic in every way**.

STAGE 5 - WAKING YOUR CLIENT

Ok, now it's time to wake you, so I'm going to count from five to one and, when I get to one, you can open your eyes and you will be wide awake and fully alert, feeling good inside, feeling better than you have felt for a long, long time... Having enjoyed this experience of hypnosis, feeling far, far better than you felt for a long, long time... feeling so good...

So here we go then... I'm going to count from five to one and, when I get to one, you can open your eyes and you will be wide awake and fully alert, feeling good inside, feeling better than you have felt for a long, long time... So here goes... 5... Slowly waking,

waking, waking...   4...   Waking a little bit more...   3... Feeling good inside...   2...   And 1!

Change your tone and increase the volume of your voice on the number "1".

NOW PRACTICE

PRACTICE

PRACTICE

CAUTION

AT THIS STAGE – **DO NOT** PRACTICE ON PEOPLE WHO ARE SUFFERING FROM DEPRESSION, ANYONE UNDER 18, ANYONE WHO IS PREGNANT OR ANYONE WITH KNOWN MENTAL HEALTH ISSUES.

THE BEST STUDENTS ARE THE ONES WHO PRACTICE THEIR SKILLS MOST.

THE MORE YOU PRACTICE, THE BETTER THERAPIST YOU WILL BECOME!

WHAT THE PEOPLE SAY:

We have built our reputation over the years based on the success of our students.

Our policy of transparency and compassion are vitally important to us as is our dedication to ensure that every single student is trained to the highest of standards.

When we asked our graduates on our dedicated Facebook group page to send us their views on the quality of our training and their own unique story of their journey to success, we were inundated with totally unbiased and honest reviews, some of which follow on the proceeding pages.

We are delighted and proud to introduce you to some of the best hypnotherapists in the whole of Europe all trained to world class standards by Innervisions School of Clinical Hypnosis.

KAREN TAYLOR: HYPNOTHERAPY ECKINGTON

I decided to train as a hypnotherapist after working as a nursery nurse for many years as well as in the community with clients and their families who needed help because they had terminal illness.

My husband passed away with a terminal illness and after several years of working in the community I decided I wanted to try a different career path as my health was suffering. I'd always had an interest in way you do things automatically and how the Brain works and functions and I'd gained lots of qualifications in psychology and emotional behavior and development whilst working with children.

After the free weekend I totally knew actually on day one the course was for me. Module one was amazing lots of practical demonstrations, videos with actual hypnotherapy sessions and comprehensive course notes. The group was friendly, lovely like minded people and we learnt so much and practiced virtually straight away. I enjoyed it and was so excited and amazed at how the techniques worked.

Any questions we had were answered by the tutor and he even helped me with some pain I was experiencing in my hip. I was so amazed by the power of hypnosis I knew this was my career path.

The course lasted 10 months. Every month we learnt so much. We were encouraged around half way though the course to practice our skills and charge a training rate which I did and I started to build up my confidence and client base with the support of the tutor who was always there to answer questions and supervise our progress. My confidence was soaring after even the first weekend.

We were given tasks throughout the course to complete. I always felt fully supported throughout all of the course and in between the monthly weekends the tutor was available to answer questions though a private group if needed.

After qualifying the support goes on though Innervisions family. There is a group for Innervisions practitioners were you can discuss issues with tutors other hypnotherapists who have all trained with this amazing school. Monthly supervision is also available, CPD with lots of interesting specialised courses and skill improvement. Working alone when you've qualified and running your own business never feels like your alone the support whether it's business advice, advice with clients, technology or anything else there is always help available. I set up my hypnotherapy practice, From the heart hypnosis and spiritual services virtually straight away after qualifying, Innervisions gave me the confidence and knowledge to do this.

LAURA CALLAGHAN: HYPNOTHERAPY BY LAURA CALLAGHAN

My road to Hypnotherapy was a very serendipitous one as if often the case. I was struggling with Post Natal Depression after the birth of my son. Counselling sent me in the direction of a past passion for yoga and it was there I discovered a hypnotherapist who inspired me.

I signed up for the Innervisions free weekend that same day. Before Hypnotherapy I worked in Events, the arts and education plus travelled... a bit of a free spirit. I had never even considered doing anything holistic before that but I think it happened at the right time of my life.

I had no idea what to expect when I attended module one that weekend in Leeds. I was really open minded and had it in my head that I was going to do this... this was the next chapter in my life. I loved that weekend, I remember practicing and thinking that it wasn't going to be as easy as I had thought it would be. It was a really informative weekend, the people I met were lovely and I still have close friends today from that weekend plus my tutor was amazing. I came away with so much new knowledge and felt like my brain was brimming over.

My tutor was fantastic and so very knowledgeable. She inspired me but also made me wonder if I could ever be as good as her. I anticipated the weekends every month excitedly and learned so very much. I began practicing on family and colleagues. That is one of the most important things I think, to practice straight away and get out there to hone your skills. There were elements of the course I enjoyed more than others, but it was fantastic overall.

It was disappointing that COVID happened in the middle of our course but it couldn't be helped and the online learning via zoom was fine. Just a shame we didn't get to celebrate at the end in the same way. The gap in the middle of my training gave me the opportunity to carry on practicing.

Post training support is fantastic. There is an absolute wealth of knowledge and helpful materials available on the Innervisions Facebook group page. You don't feel like you're alone, which you essentially are when you qualify. The other therapists in the Facebook group become your colleagues and there is no problem that they won't help you with.

There are many CPD courses that you can attend - Parts Therapy, EFT, law of attraction amongst others plus monthly supervisions and regular nuggets of wisdom in video form from Brian. Innervisions is constantly shifting and changing so you're kept abreast of everything.

There is also a lot of online support from GHR and other bodies if required. The important thing to know is that if you're ever feeling like you're alone after qualifying, just put yourself out there on the group and you'll quickly realise you're not... other therapists always offer to help and do Zoom calls with you etc.

My hypnotherapy practice has grown over the past two years. I had a goal at the beginning and I'm on track with it.

I began practicing on paying clients in May 2020 and since then I see on average three clients per week, sometimes more sometimes less.

This is fantastic for me as I also work part time for the Police. I run a small practice, but it gives me time to concentrate on the clients I do see and work towards growing my practice when my son goes to school.

Hypnotherapy has led me down a path I never expected and opened up so many doors for me in terms of personal development and better mental health. For the first time in my life I feel balanced and in touch with my unconscious mind to better be able to understand myself and find a peaceful tranquil state.#

I have learnt so many new techniques, many of which I practice on myself daily so that they almost become part of a daily routine for wellness. This has also given me a confidence which I never possessed before I started on this journey.

JAYNE PADLEY: J E CLINICAL HYPNOTHERAPY

In 2018 I had decided to plan for my retirement from nursing which I had been doing since 1983. I set out some achievable goals and planned this I studied specialist counselling diploma NLP practitioner and life coaching but I also sold my house which enabled me to pay for hypnotherapy course as I had looked into this but needed the funds. By doing all this I was investing in myself. I knew that I still wanted to offer support to people as I am both caring and compassionate. I am also only young to retire so still want to work but do something different.

Module one was unusual for me it was in the middle of covid and via zoom but still looked forward to meeting new people and the experience. I felt that to get the best out of the module and course I would put all my previous training to one side and absorb with fresh eyes all that I was being taught. I was totally hooked from the beginning thanks to the tutor and the way the course was presented. Everything was explained and demonstrated so easily and with me being open to all of this it ensured that I was free to take to the study.

The tutor was amazing very knowledgeable about the programme and had her own practice so she could draw on her own experiences and skills to educate us in the history tools and techniques also responsibilities and regulations that would be needed to be a hypnotherapist. The course was divided up into modules and could be paid for prior to each one but we had four weeks between each module to practice and do any work to be handed in which was good for me as I was still a full time nurse but it was more than manageable.

Before the course even finished the support was available and we were given all the information to help with our business our registration and development. There are monthly supervision topics which are great for Continual Professional Development (CPD) and Innervisions community for advice and support so definitely do not feel alone.

As I trained via zoom, my practice is via zoom. it is only small, and like i said at the beginning I planned for retirement so I manage my time. I focused on weight control to begin with but I am now getting clients for fears, phobias, motivation, chronic pain, confidence and so I am getting to fully utilize the tools and skills I have been taught. I only take on about 3 clients per week, that's all I need to make my living.

NICKI CLARKE: NICKI CLARK HYPNOTHERAPY

My story goes back to 1996 when I started my hypnotic journey with Innervisions School Of Clinical Hypnosis. Brian had hair then and he was my tutor 😊

I had a difficult childhood and watched my family suffer incredible trauma through a tragic accident which resulted in death.

Depression, Anxiety and addictions formed within my direct family and I was unable to help them. I buried my hand and concentrated on working full time to support my family financially and study my degree part time at Liverpool John Moore's University.

Years later I heard about a technique called hypnotherapy and loved the idea of being able to assist people through trauma without living through trauma. I worked in sales at the time so I figured that my personality would be useful in gaining rapport when I decided to pursue this dream of being able to help others. Attending this course was the best decision I ever made in my life.

I was extremely nervous about attending, I have worked from being 15 years old in retail, sales and manufacturing. The idea of being hypnotised was terrifying yet exciting but the idea of learning a skill that literally could change the way people felt or reacted was just too good to miss.

Any doubt or fear was eradicated within the first hour, I realised the people I was sat with were feeling exactly the same and the tutors were fantastic. Within the first weekend, I had learned how to hypnotise someone and experienced the wonderful feeling of hypnosis for myself.

25 years later, I'm still using the skills acquired and I am still often astounded by the results even now.

Even all those years ago, course was easy to follow and well written. The homework was interesting and practical and the encouragement to buddy up and practise with your peers was welcomed. There was just enough time between each module to allow you to practise and give you the confidence to develop your skills further

The knowledge, skills and experience of the tutor were incredible.

Brian was empathic, interesting and extremely supportive in every aspect of the learning. I can honestly say in 25 years, this course is one of the best courses I have ever taken and remains one of the most exciting, rewarding and useful courses I have ever taken.

As I studied with Innervisions 25 years ago, many changes within the course structure, facilities and support have occurred and Innervisions have evolved into a world wide leader in training. At the time you were given as much after support as required and each student was issued with all the modules and the relevant scripts.

After several years I re established contact with Innervisions and immediately without question they gave me access to all resources - something that I personally find particularly impressive - the material you are issued is incredible, the support outstanding and the access easy to manage. The team of tutors are readily available to provide any support needed and often give you more than expected and the group are familiar, friendly and supportive at all times. It's a pleasure to be in this community and I'm grateful for having found Innervisions.

I run my practise part time and focus on working with people suffering from stress, anxiety and depression. More recently I have been working with teenagers who have attended counselling and achieved minimal results. Within 2 sessions they feel like they have got their lives back and their parents are delighted. I have never had a smoker fail to stop smoking and I have worked with most phobias.

The pleasure you get from actually helping someone to improve their lives is intangible, giving them the power back never stops being amazing, being a clinical hypnotherapist is the most rewarding job in the world and I'm privileged to be a part of it.

KAREN GOODWIN: BEAUTIFUL MINDS

I had been in the hair and beauty field of work for over forty years. Within that time I had also trained in many genres of holistic therapy, including meditation. I've always been interested in the mind as I, like many people have experienced things in my life which have impacted on myself in different ways. I have been running a meditation class for a few years now, where I would take members of the class into visualisations to help them clear blocks and find peace and relaxation.

A friend of mine suggested that perhaps I would find hypnotherapy interesting. So I decided to investigate it more and came across Innervisions. As an intuitive I believe things cross your path at the right time. For me coming across Innervisions and hypnotherapy was the perfect time when I was ready to expand my knowledge. And I have loved every bit of it.

When I attended module one. I was quite nervous about stepping out of my comfort zone. But I needn't have been. The whole experience was absolutely mind blowing and left me wanting to learn more.

The people I met were all on their own journey but I felt we all had something special to offer. I felt comfortable and I found the whole experience brilliant. The way the information was given was easy to understand and just left me wanting to learn more. I left that weekend feeling excited for my new journey. And I couldn't wait to attend the next one.

The course itself I felt was interesting, informative and easy to understand. I felt it was actually a place of self discovery too. Because it allowed me to understand more about how my mind was working as well as the potential clients I would have in the future.

Every weekend brought something new and I was ready and eager to dive into learn more. My tutor made everything so interesting and I could see the passion within them for their work just made me want to be a part of that journey for myself.

I think I was already bitten by the bug so to speak. The amount of realisations you go through on the journey is mind blowing but in a positive way. And I was grateful to have such a wonderful tutor that had patience to help us all get through it in a fun and informative way. Just fabulous.

I love the post training support so much because I think this is where you can go into more depth. I love the supervision sessions and I have done many courses as extras too. The tutors are so knowledgeable and they are able to present each session in a way that I feel gives clear understanding of the subjects we cover. I think this is a vital part of becoming not just a good hypnotherapist, but becoming outstanding in your field.

My hypnotherapy practice enables me to pull all of my skills together. I work intuitively with my other therapies and have found that in some areas there is an overlap that seems to blend all of my skills together.

I love working with people to build their confidence and self esteem. Particularly with regard to anxiety and stress. Although I do cover many other areas too. And I aim to help people who see me feel at ease, this is a key area that is necessary to gain the trust between client and hypnotherapist.

I love my work and I love the transformations that can happen. My work is of service. And I am able to do this through my skills and talents as an intuitive, hypnotherapist and holistic therapist.

If I had one thing to offer to anyone who was thinking of changing direction in their lives I would say consider how much you could gain from learning and experiencing the amazing things hypnotherapy can offer. It's akin to transformation and who wouldn't want that if you could create a better life for yourself and others. Or at least guide someone else into finding it for themselves.

Love it all.

CHERYL LAWTON: MY POSITIVE HEALTH

I have spent my adult life working in healthcare as a Nurse, I'm in my 40th year. Over the years I have studied some complimentary therapies alongside the various courses I've attended in Nursing, and gaining complimentary therapies qualifications has often enhanced the care and support I have used for those in my care. For over the 40 years I have worked in a variety of specialities and healthcare settings, and most recently I have opened my own business which is a busy Ear Clinic. I see a fair proportion of my clients who have Tinnitus, which is unwanted noise that can be distressing, persistent and annoying, altering or affecting the hearing ability. One day I was particularly upset by the plight of a client, who confided in me that his Tinnitus had been so bad, that he felt like he was going mad, and was under the care of the Crisis team because he had contemplated suicide. I felt helpless and as Tinnitus is classed as permanent, I could see where he felt his options were limited, and I began to think how as an Ear clinic I could support Tinnitus Sufferers.

Some years ago I went for Hypnotherapy myself, and was treated successfully for a recurring nightmare I was having. I thought that Tinnitus too might be successfully treated as it is actually caused by the Brain. Amazingly, as this was on my mind, I saw the INNERVISIONS course advertised, and I decided to book my place. I wasn't at all wary about studying Hypnotherapy because I had been for hypnotherapy myself some years before. I had a really good outcome, which to this day has never occurred since.

Being in healthcare I was aware of various therapeutic interventions, and I was well aware of the power of the mind over the body to influence recovery and influence our health. I practiced meditation, and Reiki and was used to using my imagination in a therapeutic way, and therefore I kind of knew what to expect. I also had a friend who had done the very same course a few years before, and was pleasantly surprised how much more aware they were after it.

The INNERVISIONS course was very well put together, the topics were well organised into modules which progressed the learner deeper into the skills and techniques of hypnotherapy at just the right pace. There's an ideal balance of theory and practice it's very interactive. You can even be treated by your fellow students during the course, as you work together in the practical parts of the modules. I was released from the Bird phobia I had endured since being a child, and can now walk calmly through Pigeon flocks, and hold Owls without fear.

The way that the course is designed with attendance for one weekend every month allowed proper digestion of the course content, and resources, with time to practice the new skills and report back at the next monthly training to the Tutor and compare experiences with your peer group. The course tutors are appropriately experienced practitioners in their own right, and still actively delivering hypnotherapy in their own practices. They are able to demonstrate all the techniques and tools of hypnotherapy because they are using them and so it's all very natural and flowing. All the Tutors are trained in exactly the same way, and to all intents, with exactly the same content. INNERVISIONS uses it's own former students to teach the students of the future and in a way it's like passing down a family tradition. The process is proven over more than 25 years, and apart from minor improvements along the way, we have all received the same training.

From the moment you finish the course you are taken into the INNERVISIONS family. There are no cliques or ego's everybody has been through the same process and has most likely has had the same experiences along the way. There's a very active and supportive Facebook private group which is there 24/7 for any questions, ideas and information to be shared and responded to.

INNERVISIONS provides monthly supervision sessions which are delivered by a highly experienced team of tutors and practitioners who often have special expertise in particular areas of practice, but the sessions never seem formal or threatening the connection of the INNERVISIONS family always makes learning fun and worthwhile. CPD courses are also a means for the practitioners to learn advanced techniques that are a natural progression after the practitioner training, such as Parts Therapy, EFT, and Addictions.

I practice in Hull at my own clinic, and although I see clients for all aspects of hypnotherapy, I do specialise in supporting those with Tinnitus and have been successful in helping them to reduce and manage their condition better. I am pleased to say that one of those success stories was the original gentleman who set me on my hypnotherapy journey about 4 years ago.

MARY BLAKEY: MARY T BLAKEY THERAPY UK

I have always been intrigued by hypnotists and hypnotherapists and how hypnotherapy works and the power of the mind. I already incorporated visualisations, story telling and metaphors into my counselling practice. I saw an advert for a complimentary weekend with Innervisions and didn't think twice. After completing the complimentary weekend I was hooked and decided to train to be a hypnotherapist to compliment my business. I absolutely loved the training and became as passionate about hypnotherapy as I am about counselling. On attending module 1 I didn't know what to make of it or why anybody would offer a training weekend for free. I thought it might be a bit of a scam to be honest. However I soon realised it wasn't. The training was in a lovely hotel, with a very knowledgeable tutor, an abundance of information and with plenty of handouts. Our group was eager to learn and friendly and we were soon practising hypnotherapy on each other. Module 1 gave a lot of information about how hypnotherapy works in the brain and what hypnotherapy and being hypnotised is. The course was very informative and our tutor was amazing and as fascinating as the course content. She was very giving with her time and knowledge and made the learning fun. I honestly didn't want the course to end. Anything that she didn't already know, she took the time to find out for us. There is plenty of time to practice hypnotherapy on each other as a group which definitely helps. The course also gives help and guidance on setting up in practice and marketing. Post training there is an amazing closed Facebook group with Innervisions with an abundance of hypnotherapists from all over the country. You can post a question at any time of the day or night and within minutes a number of people will answer and will give guidance and advice on your query based on their own experience and practice. There is monthly supervision offered on line and plenty of training which is also now on line via zoom. The training is professionally delivered by Innervisions and often a book will compliment the training, sent via Amazon. You can also request a recording of the training to keep. I'm an Integrative and Client Centred Counsellor, Clinical Counselling Supervisor and a Clinical Hypnotherapist. I work creatively with adults and children. I have 16 years experience in the counselling field and in recent years added hypnotherapy to compliment my practice. Hypnotherapy uses hypnosis to work directly with the subconscious mind, facilitating you to make positive changes in your life. It can be a very quick and effective therapy which can help with a wide range of issues from phobias, trauma, anxiety, self improvement to weight loss or simply to help you to relax. I work creatively and I am very child focussed, although I also work with adults. I offer therapy at flexible times. Therapy sessions are available on line and in person.You are a unique individual and you deserve to live your best life.

JACQUELINE ANDERSON: ESSENCE HYPNOTHERAPY

Prior to being a hypnotherapist, I had been working in office management roles for over 25 years. I was approaching 50 and was feeling miserable and unfulfilled in my career so I made the decision to change direction. Office work had become mundane and boring but I had no idea what I wanted to do at that time, I felt like I was standing at a crossroads and had no idea which way to turn. Going back to college or university to retrain was out of the question as I needed to earn a full-time wage.

One evening, I just happened to be scrolling through Facebook when a post popped up about a free training weekend with Innervisions School of Clinical Hypnosis, so I requested further information. A short time after that I was contacted by one of the tutors for Innervisions and I signed up for the free weekend. After all, I had absolutely nothing to lose as the weekend was completely free.

I remember my Dad years ago talking about hypnosis as "a load of old baloney" and I have to say, I was sceptical for a while about this 'free weekend'. I had always been interested in the power of the mind and often used meditation for relaxation and studied neuroplasticity but I was a bit wary about hypnosis. Was there a hidden catch? Would there be a 'hard-selling' tactic involved to make me part with my hard-earned cash? Would I be 'hypnotised' out of money? Well fortunately, the answer to these questions is no. I was intrigued and wanted to find out more for myself, so I attended module one with a completely open mind. I have to say, I was pleasantly surprised. I took many 'gold nuggets' away with me from the free training and learned about the misconceptions surrounding hypnosis. It was a thoroughly enjoyable, fun weekend and I made the decision at the end of the second day that hypnotherapy was the way forward and I signed up for the full training course.

I started the course in 2018 but then had to defer my training for a few months due to my Dad passing away after a long illness. I re-joined for the second module in Leeds and then joined the Nottingham group with for the remainder of the course. Both tutors were brilliant, and along with my colleagues on the course they helped me through a particularly difficult time in my life. During the course my confidence improved considerably and I conquered my fear of motorway driving and flying. It was great being able to do the training at the weekend once a month, I was able to fit this in around my full-time job. I graduated with Innervisions in 2019.

There's lot's of support in the Innervisions group and also lots of opportunities for additional learning and training including new techniques and modalities. I did the EFT training, Parts training, Addictions training, Law of Attraction training and the Refresher training, to name a few. There is also the monthly supervision events that have covered a whole range of topics like training on using zoom and also marketing - which is essential for building a hypnotherapy business. There's lots of useful information on Hypnoflix.tv too, so there is support available for any issues or advice that you might need help with.

One of my favourite quotes is

"The energy of the mind is the essence of life" by Aristotle

and I decided to name my business Essence Hypnotherapy in 2019. My logo is a butterfly which symbolises transformation and resilience. In the latter part of the year I found premises in Ransom Wood, Mansfield, Nottingham. It is an idyllic place for therapies, my clinic is in a beautiful woodland setting surrounded by wildlife, it's a lovely environment to connect with nature.

The pandemic arrived shortly after I had set the business up and things were very tough for a while but we learned to pivot, adapt and evolve. As well as hypnotherapy I do EFT and alignment coaching, specialising in confidence and anxiety related issues. In the new year, my therapy dog Sirius will be joining me in the clinic, I'm really looking forward to that.

He will be providing support by helping clients with stress related issues. I left my full-time office job a few months ago to concentrate on my hypnotherapy business and now I absolutely love what I do. I have finally found my purpose in life.

PAUL TORRINGTON: EDWARD PAUL HYPNOTHERAPY

I worked as an apprentice mechanic and progressed through to Consultant Technical and then Manager. After many years I decided to change career paths and work for the NHS in a major hospital in the Clinical Engineering department, I currently still work part time there.

Part way through my motor trade years I suffered from a vertebrae problem in my lower back to which I was told was to risky to operate on and the only way forward was to take pain relief. This pain relief was in the form of high powered pain killers like tramadol, and after several years on these I became concerned of the damage they could be doing to me. So, I decided to look at alternative solutions. I did some research on hypnotherapy and it's ability to assist in this area, and had a few sessions with a chiropractor and then with a local hypnotherapist which worked fine and helped.

But mine was a long term issue, so when I saw by chance - (or was it fate?) the advertisement from 'Innervisions', for a trial weekend, I decided to take the bull by the horns and to train as a Clinical Hypnotherapist myself.

I have always genuinely loved working with people, and helping them, and being a clinical Hypnotherapist is all about helping people, and it's so rewarding when I see unfold in front of me the positive results and changes that it brings.

At first I was quite wary as unsure of what was involved or what I would actually be doing. Would I be suited to it? or indeed would I actually be capable of taking in the information and carrying out and applying what was learnt by putting the training into practice?

I needn't have worried, we were made to feel quite at ease, but also given essential ground rules that needed to be adhered to.

There were people from all walks of life, and a broad selection of age, but everyone was there for a reason, and were willing & wanted to learn.

The course was really constructive, open to discussion in depth, with lots of practical hands on work. even at that early stage I could see and feel that we were starting to gel into a 'Hypno family' - everyone supported each other, shared life experiences, & I feel developed into better people.

The training is quite intense at times and can be mentally exhausting too, but it was always enjoyable. Our Tutor really was excellent! he lived and breathed the training, and put 100% into everything. He made it fun, but was also quite serious in the places he needed to be.

He put the training into bite size chunks, and offered up examples, if we were struggling with anything in particular he would take time to ensure this was rectified.

The post training support is excellent! Complimented with regular supervision and study sessions on a wide variety of subjects. These regularly include a guest a speaker.

But, there is also actually so much resource and support that is available and readily given by everyone on the Innervisions therapy community site. This site has become invaluable, we can run ideas by each other, share experiences, gain ideas and more knowledge, it really is a big Innervisions hypnotherapy family.

I currently run my sessions from a room at home as I have ample parking, privacy & access, in comfortable and relaxing surroundings. In summer it's even possible to conduct them outside in a quiet garden area overlooking fields & countryside. but also occasionally I go mobile to a clients own home as a number of people seem to prefer this initially.

I've have great success with various issues. For example sleep problems, stress, anxiety, to sports enhancements and concentration, pain management exam revision, fear of flying/driving etc etc to name a few. advise.

HELEN JANE: HELEN JANE HYPNOTHERAPY

Whilst working for British Airways as long-haul cabin crew I sustained a serious back injury which resulted in surgery. I was referred to a pain management specialist to help with the chronic pain. After a few sessions I was pain free. I didn't know it at the time however this was my first experience of hypnosis. As a result of the injury, I was forced to change career and decided to retrain as a life coach and mental health practitioner. I loved working with people with mental health issues using my life coaching and Cognitive Behavioural Therapy skills whilst they waited for counselling. Over time I noticed that many people came back into service with the same issues time after time or that counselling, CBT, and life coaching just did not help. It became apparent that, for some, additional support was needed. I started to research and became fascinated with the power of the unconscious mind. This led to me deciding to train as a hypnotherapist so that I could work with my clients on a deeper level to make lasting change.

I was excited to attend module one. I was open minded and intrigued. Having already researched hypnotherapy and having experienced the benefit of hypnosis in pain management I was curious if I would be able to incorporate hypnotherapy into my practice to support my clients. My main concern was how I would fit the training in around working full time. After learning how the modules were delivered, I decided this would not be an obstacle to my training to become a hypnotherapist.

I really enjoyed attending module one. It was helpful to meet the tutor and to gain insight into the training. Any concerns that students had were fully addressed and I felt so confident in the Innervisions' training that I signed up without hesitation.

The course is very well structured. It takes you on a pathway from no knowledge to having the confidence, skills, and knowledge to set up a hypnotherapy practice.

Having the monthly sessions enabled me to work through the content at my own pace and then bring any questions to the sessions. There was no such thing as a stupid question.

Throughout the training I felt fully supported and encouraged by the tutor. The tutor was very knowledgeable and supportive and brought valuable experience of running her own successful practice to the sessions.

The content was delivered professionally and at an appropriate pace.

There were plenty of opportunities to ask questions and ample time for practice sessions to help build confidence. I particularly enjoyed the workshops which meant that I had the tools and the confidence to begin running sessions as soon as I had qualified.

The post training support has been excellent. It really does feel as though you are part of a family. It is so helpful to be able to tap into the experience and support of other more experienced hypnotherapists.
There is ample opportunity to attend additional trainings to further your knowledge and refresher training to brush up on your skills should you need it.

Opportunities for monthly supervision with expert speakers are offered which are also very helpful.

I feel totally supported in the knowledge that I can ask for advice and support when needed.

I love working with midlife women.

Midlife can be a challenging time for many women with lots of changes, both expected and unexpected. Women often feel stuck, lost, unseen and unheard, unsure of the way forward as they deal with lack of purpose, burnout, health issues, relationship breakdown, empty nesting, bereavement, career change and redundancy.

Over the years I have worked with 100's of women using a variety of therapies including hypnotherapy, life coaching, EFT and energy alignment to support them in moving forward.

I offer a bespoke service tailored to the needs of the individual. This often includes work around menopause, weight management, health issues, pain management, anxiety, stress, confidence, and sleep. I also offer group sessions and online courses.

DONNA GALLOWAY: SEVEN HILLS WELLBEING CENTRE

Previously I worked as a sales merchandiser for a blue-chip company for many years. Life was becoming very repetitive and uninteresting. Therefore, I needed to do something about it. I decided to change career for a more fulfilled lifestyle. I saw the Innervisions School of Clinical Hypnosis advertisement on Facebook and something clicked. I was intrigued. As the first workshop was free I thought that I would give it a go. It wasn't going to cost me anything for the weekend except time.

However, I didn't expect to be so pleasantly surprised and pleased with the weekend course and waited with anticipation to hear if I had been accepted into the full course.

On the first morning of the free weekend, I felt so nervous and I must admit even a little sceptical. I had always enjoyed the hypnotist on TV and was about to find out more about the secrets of the hypnotic world.

Little did I know that I was about to change my life forever. The other students on the course were from all different walks of life. Different abilities and reasons for being there. However that didn't matter at all, they were a very friendly group of people. The free foundation weekend was well put together, informative, enjoyable and the weekend went very fast. We learned of the history of hypnotherapy and the misleading information regarding the subject. We even got to practice on each other.

I can't praise the course enough really, it was a 10 month course packed with lots of reading, discussions, practical exercises and sessions.

During the course we developed the skills needed to competent and confident hypnotherapists. You could ask the tutor any questions and they be answered fully from a knowledgeable tutor. The only silly question is the one you don't ask.' This is so true. It really didn't matter how many we asked, so long as we understood. Some of the people I met on the course have become very good friends and the ones who lived further afield, there's always Facebook. After you graduate and set up your business, it can be quite daunting. However once qualified you will be invited into a private group for professional hypnotherapists. This group is invaluable. The camaraderie, kindness and helpfulness of those who are in the group never ceases to amaze me. There is always someone online to help you though your questions and advise you on the best way to help your clients and business. Even if you don't have a question to ask, following the conversation on different approaches and subjects reinforces the training you received during the course. I'd definitely recommend that you join the group once invited.

I had a wish to open my own Wellbeing Centre. A place for all different holistic therapies with Hypnotherapy being the main practice. Fortunately I have now achieved that. It was a 3 year journey from first seeing the perfect building for my venture, as someone else ran a business from there, to now being proud of what I have achieved. I am privileged to be able to help clients change their lives, see the difference in clients from walking in with despair and after hypnotherapy sessions take back control of their own lives.

VIVIENNE RAWNSLEY:

Working in education, as a teacher in both special needs and mainstream schools, for over 30 years I had developed an interest in the workings of the human mind and how events from the past can get locked in our subconscious mind affecting the choices we make in the present and the future. Having personally experienced the impact of hypnosis following a traumatic divorce I expanded my learning further and decided to train as a clinical hypnotherapist.

Training as a hypnotherapist gave me a key to unlocking the power of our subconscious minds and transform life as we know it.

I attended the first weekend training sessions with an open mind as an opportunity to further my personal and professional development. During module one the experience I had being hypnotised together with training I had engaged in as a neuro linguistic programming practitioner fell into place. I was excited by what I was learning and drawn further into the world of clinical hypnotherapy. The tutor and training material were informative and engaging.

This supported my decision of, rather than enrolling in an online course offering no post qualification support or business development training, to enrol with the INNERVISIONS school of clinical hypnosis.

I found the INNERVISIONS training to be extremely high quality. The combination of theory and practical sessions, during which each student experienced and used each technique and process, was a great combination and supported each of the trainees in gaining confidence as they became clinical hypnotherapists. Working together developed the skills of each individual as the high quality tutor monitored the practical application of the theory that he had shared with us. The course material was easy to access for all learning styles with additional support for those trainees who felt less confident in their abilities. Each student experienced elements of the hypnosis training and this impacted their confidence and other areas of their personal development.

Post training support has included opportunities to engage in supervision as required by the General Hypnotherapy Council.

Additional training has also been available as support for gaining additional skills in specific areas. These have included both hypnosis techniques and business development. Training that I have engaged in has included Law of Attraction, Emotional Freedom Technique, Addictions, Parts Therapy, How to use Facebook and Facebook adds, Using audible to create professional hypnosis recordings using audible and Hypnoslimmer. I work with clients both face to face and online to support them in experiencing change in their lives. Much of the work I do involves overcoming trauma. This ranges from small seemingly insignificant incidents that have impacted the clients subconscious mind to affect how they regard themselves and their world, to life changing events that shake the clients world result in them struggling to exist beyond it. Hypnotherapy is blended with other tools to create bespoke packages that support the clients in making changes in their lives, resulting in increased confidence, happiness, personal and professional opportunities, satisfaction and success.

MICHELE KNOTT SIMEY: HYPNOTHERAPY BY MICHELE KNOTT SIMEY

After absolutely hating school for the whole of my childhood, I somehow found myself as a teaching assistant. With 11 years under my belt a change in management found me questioning my commitment to teaching. I was always the "go to" person for comfort and advice so I started to consider retraining as a counsellor or therapist. I wasn't really sure which course to take or where to look for guidance so I decided to rely on my instincts and wait for a "sign" to help me decide. It wasn't too long before I noticed a post on social media regarding Innervisions hypnotherapy training. I read and reread the advert and something just clicked. I enquired the very next day. After a chat with the course tutor over the phone, I was invited to attend a free training weekend at a local hotel. When I arrived at the venue I met several other people and we got chatting. We all wondered what we might expect but I just had a good feeling about it. The tutor called us through, introduced herself and explained the shape of the weekend before allowing us all to get acquainted over refreshments. On that very first morning I knew I'd found my path, I belonged. The whole weekend flew by in what seemed like seconds, I was hooked. The best part of course was it was completely free!

My tutor was Lynn Appleyard, a brilliantly engaging teacher who puts across content in such a way that you barely notice that you're being educated. The modules are absolutely fascinating and I can honestly say I've never enjoyed a course as much as this one.

We all qualified together in a lovely party atmosphere in the hotel, followed by a celebratory dinner in a local hostelry! Post qualification, we were all transferred from our original media support group to the amazing Innervisions group. I for one have used the group for advice and I hope I've also given support. It's also a great place tell each other about our wins! All of the supervision opportunities are posted within the group and delivered via Zoom. This makes things accessible for all. What's also great is that all of the course tutors hang out in the group ready to impart their extensive knowledge whenever we may falter.
As soon as I was confident in my ability I left my day job and set up my therapy room at home. I wanted the space to feel calm and comfortable and with a sumptuous chair, soft throws, beautiful artwork and peaceful music I achieved my dream. I now work with people who suffer from anxiety, low self esteem, insomnia, lack of confidence, who would like to stop smoking or would like to weigh less. I just love being a hypnotherapist and have never once looked back.

I'm so glad that Brian Glenn decided he wanted to help a million people and although he may have meant hypnotherapy clients, indirectly I am one of his million! Thanks Brian x

SUE FERGUSON: SUE FERGUSON HYPNOTHERAPY

I am a nurse who still works part time so deal with people from a physical model. I always felt like there was more to life than just physical health and quite by accident I came upon the free weekend with Innervisions . I was intrigued by the content of the course and also by the others who attended that free weekend. Something was ignited within me , I could sense this was the answer to what I was looking for so decided to sign up for the course.

My fellow students , along with the fabulous tutors soon turned my life upside down. I found out more about myself in those months of training than I knew existed!!! The training changed me as a person (for the better) and gave me amazing skills that I now use not only with my hypnotherapy clients but I also apply the knowledge that the mind is capable of so much more than we possibly give it credit for in dealing with patients.

To use the skills to help an individual to change their life and to see life from a different perspective is truly a gift . All thanks to Innervisions.

I was the tutors worse nightmare as I was so sceptical. I asked so many questions and challenged just about everything. I was probably the most annoying student in the room. As a nurse the things that were presented to me sort of challenged my perception of life and the 'way things were'. I found the other students intriguing, so many different people with such different view points and beliefs. I was sure I wouldn't have anything in common with them. How wrong I was about everything. They became good friends , we all shared a lot, both in the lecture rooms and out !!!! I grew as a person and quite honestly can say the course changed me for the better and I haven't looked back since.

I wouldn't be the person I am today without the Innervisions course and I even got the certificate for the most improved student 😊

My tutors were so enthusiastic about the course content. They delivered it in an easy to understand and enlightening way. Their knowledge and enthusiasm was infectious, making each weekend informative and fun. We did have so much fun!!! I can honestly say I looked forward to each weekend with delight.

The content of the course was presented in a professional manner and full information was given as to what to expect, what was expected of you and how to achieve the best in yourself.

Being able to put into practice what you had learned each weekend was invaluable . The practical work and theory were complimentary.

Once qualifying it's a scary thing to start seeing clients initially but the best aspect of Innervisions is the support provide on line with the Innervisions support group . You are able to post queries about anything without the fear of being judged . You gain insight into others practice just by reading the different posts from newly qualified and those who have been around a bit longer. No question is too big or too small and you are never made to feel like your question is irrelevant. Lots of information about courses, supervision, and articles are provided to access continuously. You feel as if you are not alone as you go along your own journey.

I only see a few clients at the moment as I still work as a nurse part time.

I have a small converted room at home which I currently use as a therapy room . I am having an extension built to provide more space . I see a whole range of client issues from slimming to anxiety, from stopping smoking to IBS.

Clients are generally from word of mouth (I do find the marketing aspect slightly daunting) I have developed my own programme for IBS symptom relief and am keen to specialise in this area of hypnotherapy. I would like to eventually give up nursing to devote more time to my hypnotherapy clients.

CAROLLE WESTBURY: INSIDE MIND HYPNOTHERAPY

I loved the idea of helping a variety of people through the wonderful world of hypnotherapy. I have always been the person where people have gravitated to for emotional and practical help, and eventually realised that this was what one of my highest values was. It gives me great pleasure to be involved, and to meet such a variety of people. Who are each fascinating in their own individual ways. The sense of satisfaction when a person has been set free from an issue or problem that has previously been hampering their happiness and well being is second to none. My career has previously been is sales management which is in essence fulfilling a customers needs, and I believe hypnotherapy has a similar purpose.

I attended module one feeling very nervous, but curious about learning about the world of hypnotherapy. It was an enlightening and enjoyable experience, which gave a fascinating insight into the human brain. I did think that I would probably only attend for one day of the two day course, but I can honestly say I was hooked after the initial introduction and could not wait to attend day two. On the second day we were taken deeper into the training and given wonderful insights into hypnotherapy and its power. The end of that day was completed with a practical demonstration which was truly awe inspiring.

On my course we unfortunately lost our initial trainer, but the transition to our new trainer Laura was absolutely seamless, and I felt completely supported throughout the whole process. We were informed at the very beginning of the course that our lives would change as a result of the course, and how true that information was!

There is plenty of support after qualification. With an online community, and direct messaging to anyone within the group. There are regular supervision courses via zoom, and there is also forums for discussion and assistance. There are also other courses on offer which enable one to delve deeper into subjects such as parts therapy, addictions, and pain management. At the end of the course and on the last weekend of graduation we were advised how to set up a hypnotherapy practice, and guided towards the correct bodies with which to be involved in. There is always someone to turn to for advice and help. The family of Innervisions hypnotherapy is certainly very embracing and supportive.

My practice is conducted both face to face and via zoom. I'm happy to work in whatever way is best for my clients. Although I am perfectly happy to treat a variety of problems and issues, the majority of my work so far has been in the area of fears and phobias. I am very grateful and humbled to have quite a lot of recommendations in this sphere, and my clients are certainly ecstatic to shed unwanted thoughts and feelings.

EAH GOODALL: LEAH GOODALL HYPNOTHERAPY

I have spent the first 25 years of my career in finance, specifically debt chasing and I enjoy driving fast cars in my spare time and part time. During those years I met my wonderful husband who is an ex royal marine commando. Over the years the signs of PTS(d) began to show in him but soldiers don't often talk and almost always refuse therapy, it's ingrained in them to 'crack on'. I sought out a therapy that could help him where almost nothing needs to be said, just a few small positive solution focused questions. I found hypnotherapy. I found Innervisions School of clinical hypnosis. The free weekend changed my life. I attended the free weekend in Nottingham in 2013 with an open mind and a hope that I had found a solution. The energy in the room over the weekend is amazing. The structure of the course is well laid out and very easy to understand and follow and the more you learn the more exciting the day becomes. The tutors are amazing, funny and so full of knowledge, able to answer even the most bizarre questions. It didn't feel like school, it was fun and entertaining right through to the end and i walked away knowing how to perform hypnosis. I was very blessed to be able to return to the school a few years later and aid one of the diplomas alongside my former tutor. I trained at the lace market. The rooms were very large and clean with excellent facilities, tea, coffee, juice, biscuits and cakes all laid on. Our tutor brought the science behind the myths, the facts and evidence and headed the classes. The students I trained with are from all around the world which brought amazing insight into cultural beliefs and different kinds of clients that may walk through our doors. We practiced on each other and as a result have all become life long friends who meet regularly for social CPD. The thing that I love most about my training with Innervisions is that it never ended, I joined a family. The online support that we all give each other is second to none. We all join other groups but the skill level of the therapists through the years, the monthly supervision, the more in depth subjects, watching each other bloom and choose paths to specialise in, the sharing of clients, therapy swapping with each other, the list of support is endless.

I have been seeing hypnotherapy clients for 9 years now. I don't advertise. I enjoy being out on the open roads so I have a part time day job driving fast cars and I see all of my clients by referral only. I started small with friends and family as trust was already there, who went on and told their friends and family and now I see 4 clients a week, because I choose to. Financially I've never been able to say that before. I set aside 8 hours over two days. I have converted a bedroom in my home into my studio and I visited local therapists with clinics and sourced places that felt right for me and my clients. I specialise with depression, anxiety, PTS(d) and stress related clients but really enjoy the journeys I take with my HypnoSlimmer clients, their results are always so amazing. I'm not conventional, I don't ask for reviews and with weight change its so easy to see it happen it lifts my soul.

KELLY KING: BE FREE CLINICAL HYPNOTHERAPY

I was diagnosed with a genetic condition and suffered crippling chronic health from the age of 40, & early onset menopause. I enrolled with Innversions in 2019 to make changes to my health and life. As I learnt, I healed, then I wanted to help others through my new knowledge and life experience. Sadly Covid held me back and knocked my confidence and self esteem. It's coming to the end of 2021, Covid is still prevalent, but it's no longer holding me back. I am now in a position to offer my hypnotherapy services as an on-line therapist or in person.

I went along to the free foundation weekend in Sheffield during September, thinking I wasn't good enough or even clever enough and full of self doubt and limiting beliefs. But I should have left all of that doubt at the front door. I had the most amazing weekend. I was absolutely buzzing. I had seen the most amazing things happen, there, right in front of my eyes. I loved everything about the weekend, the like minded people who were there with me. The quality of information, the delivery of the information, the demonstrations, everything. Quite simply, I was hooked, line and sinker.

I absolutely loved the professional relationship I had with my tutor. He and his assistant, presented and assisted the course with maximum effect. Nothing was too much trouble to re-explain or offer a more in-depth explanation at any stage. Our homework, course work and practice sessions, were always of a high professional standard, with enough time or more if needed, to practice to the fullest extent. He was professional at all times, friendly, approachable and full of hypnotherapy life experience and knowledge. There was always an opportunity to ask him anything and he would always guide and support us where necessary.

The post training experiences have been to the highest standard with Brian and or members of his team. I have undertaken a hypnotherapy refresher course to boost my confidence and self esteem (due to graduating during Covid) and further training with the Emotional Freedom Technique course and the Law of Attraction course which were both amazing and have given me the opportunity to use with clients. This is a very exciting time for me. I now see Covid as a pause in my life and practice, whereby I had the opportunity to gain extra experience and more knowledge from Inversions. I am launching my new hypnotherapy practice (post covid) to help my wider community and also specialising in midlife issues, The Menopause and past Traumas.

A very warm thank you to Brian for being a part of his amazing warm Innervisions family. I know that I can come to Brian and his Team and/or the Facebook Group with any query or question and I know it will be answered quickly with a resolution.

LEANNE DEWEY: MADE MINDSET

The power of the mind has always intrigued me, I truly believe with the right mindset that anything is possible!

Hypo-Coaching is tied with practical strategies and powerful and effective techniques, adding another dimension to traditional hypnotherapy and coaching.Work ing with both the conscious and subconscious mind allows you to make deeper, longer lasting changes, from the inside out. My passion has always been to help people, who are ready to help themselves and this absolutely can do that! I attended module one with an open mind and saw it as an learning weekend, I'm a sucker for courses so was not something new to me. The weekend was very informative and I learnt so much over the two days, when I got home I started consuming as much information as I could about the power of hypnosis and it didn't take me long to know this was the path for me!

I loved that the course was offered as a free weekend to begin and there was no pressure to join which to me is a good quality.

The course in general is very good, there is plenty to learn and an array of areas covered. There is definitely enough material to set up your practice and get going straight after the course including the relevant business information needed. I liked the variety of practical and theory learning, the balance was just right to allow you to gain the knowledge needed but also build confidence in your own ability as an hypnotherapist. Our tutor was very helpful and supportive to everyone on the course - I do like to ask a lot of questions and he was able to answer everyone I had :)

After the training we was invited to join the community group which has many files, scripts that can aid you in your own business. There is also the support to ask questions and get other peoples points of view and there recommendations which is a real nice to have if you are presented with a pain point that you haven't had much experience with in the past. I'm an Internationally Accredited Transformation Coach, Accredited Clinical Hypnotherapist, Mum and Life Junkie!

I specialise in helping self-doubting women who know they want more, find their confidence and self worth, remove limiting beliefs that are holding them back and develop a powerful mindset that works for them!

I'm obsessed with helping ladies all over the world reach their full potential whilst enjoying the journey to get there. I help my clients achieve their personal goals on a 1:1 basis, with my full support and accountability I promise you, that you can too achieve whatever in life you want, on your own terms!

EQUAL OPPORTUNITIES

All applicants will receive consideration for a place on our Practitioner Level Training Course without regard to race, colour, religion, gender, gender identity or expression, sexual orientation, national origin, genetics, disability, age, or veteran status.

Whilst academic qualifications may be an advantage, we regard it as only being a small part of the learning curve to becoming a competent clinical hypnotherapist. This hypnotherapy training course is therefore open to those with a genuine interest in hypnotherapy even though they may not have any relevant prior learning or training.

As a caring training provider, it is not uncommon for us to allow certain people to attend our course at a reduced fee, or even free of charge if we feel they have the life skills and passion that is conducive to our profession, but do not have the financial resources to pay. Please note however that this is strictly at the discretion of the tutor and Principal and free and subsidised places will only be awarded if we feel the student meets our strict criteria.

Please also note that the student will be protected by our strict codes of confidentiality.

WHAT NEXT?

Every single day, Hypnotherapists worldwide are making a massive impact on the lives of fellow human beings by helping them resolve the wounds and struggles of modern day living.

Furthermore; by becoming a Clinical Hypnotherapist, you get to play in the fascinating space of human potential. You get to explore the power of the human mind and witness what it can do to overcome physical, mental and emotional concerns. And as part of this process, you will evolve as a human being yourself.

Having enjoyed and completed our Free Foundation Weekend, you are now welcome to continue your training to practitioner level.

Secure your place now on the following link:

www.innervisions.co.uk/practitioner

Printed in Great Britain
by Amazon

35632888R00066